When Flowers Speak

Dwayne Cole

Parson's Porch Books

When Flowers Speak
ISBN: Softcover 978-1-960326-27-0
Copyright © 2023 by Dwayne Cole

Parson's Porch Books is an imprint of Parson's Porch *&* Company (PP*&*C) in Cleveland, Tennessee. PP*&*C is a self-funded charity which earns money by publishing books of noted authors, representing all genres. Its face and voice is **David Russell Tullock** (dtullock@parsonsporch.com).

Parson's Porch *&* Company *turns books into bread & milk* by sharing its profits with the poor.

www.parsonsporch.com

When Flowers Speak

Preface

In the depth of winter I finally learned that there was in me an invincible summer.—Albert Camus

As I walked in the Beauty and Wonder of Alaska in the last decade, flowers spoke to me, saying, "Take my picture. Write a poem about me." Flowers are never isolated, but are connected with everything that is before them, beside them, under them, and over them. Flowers both clothe and reveal the spirit of nature. A flower poem is nature magically revealing itself. I often capitalize Beauty, Wonder, Tenderness, and Kindness as names for God. At a time when the name, God, is abused and associated with a conservative judgmental spirit, these poems allow me to speak a daisy fresh freeing message.

Most of the flower poems were written in the depth of Alaska winters, a time of almost total darkness. This adventurous activity, created in me an invincible spring and summer. Photos and poems bring their own sunshine that warms our soul. Flowers speak Tenderness and the magic of Wonder.

Globe Opening

The world evolved
One flower at a time
Kissed by Tenderness

"There is a voice that doesn't use words - Listen!" ~RUMI

All are included in Beauty,
for Beauty is Infinity.

Flowers contain the world
sun is at the center of them.

Flower petals open to sun,
shine on all with loving care.

"Don't wait for someone to bring you flowers.
Plant your own garden and decorate your own soul."
—Luther Burbank

With freedom, books, flowers, and the moon, who could not be happy?
—Oscar Wilde

Garden Dreaming...

I have my flowers,
and I have my poetry.
What more could I ask?

Contemplative Walking

According to my iPhone app, each year for the last decade,

I have walked an average of 5 miles per day in the beauty of Alaska.

Hearing nature say, "Take my picture, and write a poem about me."

My walking is a form of meditative exercise. While I walk, I am

contemplating the Goodness of Life and the Beauty of Nature.

In these moments, I dive all the way in, beyond the ordinary,

to the deeper source of thought and pure Divine Consciousness.
I am enlarged every time I transcend from the temporal
to the eternal, from mortal to immortal. I come back refreshed,
filled with Tenderness I have gathered from the wildflowers,
birds, and alpenglow mountain views. I prayerfully move through the
day with renewed enthusiasm for enjoying the precious gift of Life
with family and friends.

> To see the world evolving,
> one flower at a time.
>
> Blossom in Beauty and Wonder—
> The human heart bouquet.
>
> Is to hold Infinity in your hands,
> Eternity in your soul.

*****

> Photos are poems
> And poems are photos
> A flower garden

This book, *When Flowers Speak,* is a flower garden
waiting to decorate your life with Beauty and Wonder.
The garden has been planted and nurtured
for the last decade.

Take the book to a quiet place
and let it decorate your soul.

Photo by my life-long friend, G. W. Reid who has blossomed into heaven

In the garden
Hear flowers singing
Discover your song

In poetry
Nature completes itself
As civilization

The world has evolved,
one flower at a time.

Butterflies sipping nectar,
bees singing the first love songs.

All nature comes alive—
Humans join the symphony.

*****

To see the world in a flower,
heaven in a butterfly.

Is to be held in God's hands—
Eternity in our soul.

The One in many,
The many in One.

Fireweeds are flowers
Baptized by purifying fire
Heaven's stars shining
When painted by loving hands
Framed for all to see

*****

Fireweed petals fall
Spreading soft purple blankets
Stars shine in moon light

An Ode to Love

I knew the first day I saw you,
an adventure was under way.

Two flowers blossoming
in a duet of love.

Dancing in warm sunshine.
Side by side for eternity.

Photo by Sandra Felix

Two Hearts Become One

My soul thrilled upon seeing
this heart shaped flower.
I wanted to step out of my body
and burst into blossom.
Become enfolded with you as one,
in our Garden of Eden home.
Valentines forever!

"Look at flowers, butterflies, trees, and children
with the eyes of compassion. Compassion will
change your life and make it wonderful."
—Thích Nhất Hạnh

Spring flowers are only for a season
unless their name is grandchild.

Flowers, grandchild's smile
Bright sun shiny day. What else
Could my soul desire!

A grandchild's bright smile,
a bouquet of wildflowers—
Heaven in my heart.

Where do flowers end
and grandchild begin?
Both a bouquet of love.

It's not about
The flowers you bring to us.
It's the flower you are.

Eternity Blossoms

The world was created,
one flower at a time.

Butterflies sipping nectar,
bees singing the first love songs.

All nature comes alive—
Humans join the chorus.

Oh yellow sunlight,
Flower of heaven's joy.
Sing our soul awake.

In your bright eyes,
sleeping loved ones come awake—
Flowers blossoming!

See the sun rise.
Cup a flower in your hand.
Become a star!

Hold Infinity in your heart.
Eternity in your soul.

Drink the Cup of Joy

Today the fireweed
is wearing its red blouses— Open for the bees.
Oh to nuzzle that sweetness.
Grateful for the gift given.

Gratitude

Today the fireweed is blazing.
Wearing its red blouses open.

Open for the bees to nuzzle—
Sweetness and nourishment for hive.

Baskets filled with sweetness—
Grateful for gift given.

Water lilies open,
giving birth to the sun.

Snow cricket's chirping.
My heart beating in response.

Blue heron fishing for minnows—
A joy filled day.

*****

Two little snow crickets
ride in water lily boat.

Softly swaying, bouncing,
enjoying nectar ecstasy.

Food of angels and elves—
Lily pad blessing

I smile with the frogs
And find in lilies a Beauty
Too deep for words

*****

Their castle in the pond,
    the little cricket frogs adore.

They ride in the lily pad boat,
    and wooing music make.

White lily, symbol of purity,
    beautiful eyes winking love.

In nature we never see anything isolated, but everything in connection with
something else which is before it, beside it, under it and over it.
—Johann Wolfgang von Goethe

Walking in the garden,
I pause at the giant sunflower.

It has burned through its mask,
fully open to the sun.

I become one with the bee,
One with the sun shining on me.

Fireweed blossoms fall

On the tundra mountain side

Stars in the twilight

*****

Fireweed blossoms fall,

on the tundra mountain side.

Blouses open for caressing—

Bees nuzzling the sweetness.

Stars in the twilight, The

Milky Way!

Humans evolved in
a bio-centric world
We are all flowers

When I view flowers
the world becomes a flower.
I am a flower.
My mother is a flower
sharing kindness with me.

*****

When we view pansies—
The world becomes a flower.

Our mothers are flowers,
sharing kindness with us.

In Eden, we are all flowers—
Remember to be kind.

Frank Green photo

Lily Pond Magic

When lilies blossom
The whole world is a flower
Love comes to kiss us

*****

When lilies blossom
Beauty too great for words
Is born in our soul

27

Photosynthesis

All life is inter-related,
　　　inter-connected as one.

You cannot cup a flower,
　　　without touching a star.

Stars in the sky live and die—
　　　There is star dust in our soul.

*****

Flowers changed the world,
　　　one petal at a time.

To cup a flower in hand
　　　is to touch Infinity.

Stars in the sky live and die—
　　　There is star dust in our soul.

Photo by G. W. Reid

Soul Awakening

When I contemplate in Nature,
   I feel my soul ripening .

Opening to the beauty of God,
   the Poet of the world.

Flowers blossom in the garden,
   bees and butterflies sing to me.

*****

Oh Poet, put down your pen.
   No more writing of words.

The bees and butterflies
   have their own alphabet.

Simply be still and let
   the flowers speak the poem.

Teach kindness for all.

In the Old Testament, God spoke to Moses and asked him to tell the Israelites to make tassels on the corners of their garments, to help them to remember all the commandments and to keep them as a sign of holiness. (Numbers 15:37-40). In the New Testament Gospel of Matthew, Jesus used flowers as a symbol of God's care. (Matthew 6:28-34). Mother Teresa picked up children abandoned in the night on Calcutta streets and brought them to her clinic for healing. Buddha said, my teaching is kindness.

> Sit among flowers,
> Touch Jesus' robe of God's love.
>
> Sit among flowers,
> Touch Mother Teresa's robe of compassion.
>
> Sit among flowers,
> Touch Buddha's robe of kindness.

Come to my garden
Flowers walk and flowers talk
Be still and listen
Do you hear them whispering
Love songs from my heart to yours

Little Flowers

"Let the beauty we love be what we do.
There are hundreds of ways to kneel and kiss the ground."
— Rumi

Pansies/violets
have such lovely faces
Beauty in all faces

Photo by Robert Y. Sandford

I bow before the orange velvet daylily
with heart ripened by divine Beauty.
Wrapped in Eden's enlivened gifts.
Lips wet with Muses' nectar,
my soul sings joyfully.

Nature fills my heart with love
and I grow more compassionate
toward all people of all nations.
And desire to preserve Beauty
and Goodness for all to enjoy.

Photo by G. W. Reid

I laugh with butterflies
And find in flowers a Beauty
Too deep for words

God cares for the birds
And the flowers of the fields
Cares for you and me

Heaven opens
Angels coming to inspire
Heaven and earth One

Wings of Inspiration
Link heaven and earth
Ladder to heaven

Gifts from heaven
Seeing Beauty in all
Mystical union

(When the word, heaven, occurs in my poems, I mainly use the word to
refer to a higher consciousness that is within us, much like
the ancient Chinese philosopher, Confucius).

We cannot touch the sun.
    The sun touches the world with warmth.

Look what happens
    to a love like that.

Calls flowers to open.
    Spreads sweet aroma in the air.

Calls souls to awake.
    Fills with Beauty and Goodness.

God cares for the birds
and God cares for you.

D. Cole

Bluebirds and flowers
soften our hearts, giving life.
Heaven blossoms!

(A colored pencil drawing I did while teaching
this poetic-art to our grandchildren.)

Snow covered peaks
Littered with twinkling star dust
Fragrance of flowers
Weave our lives as a necklace
Make us a flower garden

I write poems
Longing for eternity
Give life back to God

In religion of past
Saints performed miracles
To prove faith in God
I need no tricks to prove Love
Love words and kind actions are fine

Snow covered peaks
Littered with twinkling star dust
Fragrance of flowers

Scintillating
Raindrops falling on pink skin
Touched by heaven's glow

Undreamed Beauty
A halo around the sun
Wakes consciousness
Enlarges our life meaning
Gives enlivenment

In this Beauty
The world sings itself awake
Our soul sings its part
The light of transformation
A symphony of Love

God is the Poet of the world
with tender patience leading
by a vision of truth, beauty, and goodness.
—Alfred North Whitehead

We cannot touch the sun
The sun touches world with warmth

Look what happens
to a love like that

Calls flowers to open
Spread sweet aroma in the air

God is in the sun and flowers
Touching in tender ways

Calling souls to awake
Spread Beauty and Goodness

Crossing all boundaries of race and sex
Inclusive Love for all

Flowers come in many forms
Pansies, bunnies, butterflies
Nature's magic wand

I bring a present
The sweetest I could find
Blossom kisses

Ode to Summer

I rise early to
Walk in verdant valleys
To feel new Life

Flowers are blooming
Birds gather food for nestlings
Life is starting over

I step more lively
Start singing a happy tune
Summertime magic

Eternal things originate in silence. —Dwayne Cole

Life became frenzied
She went into her garden
Whispered to flowers
She became a butterfly
and her mind was calmed

"Deep in their roots, all flowers keep the light." –Theodore Roethke

Rooted in darkness
All through the long winter nights
Flowers keep the light
In spring they burst forth in brilliance
Inspiring us to rise and shine

Sit among flowers
Touch the heart of God. D. Cole

Spring flowers laughing
Tickled by the bees sipping nectar
Sweet as honey

Cole Thomas Photo

Glowing moonlight skin
Shining through sheer nightgown
Flowers blossom

The sunflower is Ukraine's national flower.
Since Russia invaded Ukraine,
it has become a global symbol of unity
and hope from people around the world.

Oh yellow sunlight
Flower of golden heaven
Sing world soul awake

Ukraine, a Flower
We cup in compassion
See Hope rise

Floating like lilies
Bouquets from heaven's bright shore
Gifts of happiness

Oh to be a bee
First trip from the honeycomb
Fall in flower cup

Alaska's state flower
Spirit of the early settlers
Forget-me-not

After the fires
Fields are turning green again
Fireweed blossoms
A miracle glowing
A resurrection for sure

Fireweed Wonder

What would it be like
To sway in gentle breeze
In field of fireweed

Having bees
Flutter and buzz
While sipping nectar

Giving sweetness to tongue
Feel the flutter of wings
floating away with life for the hive

Time stands still
When gazing at flowers
Flowers speak forever

Life framed by flowers
A great adventure for sure
Filled with wonder

Shown spring flowers
Red, yellow, purple delights
Child opens mouth
Become a child to enter
Glory of Heaven's ways

Bleeding heart flowers
inspire Kindness toward all
Purple butterfly

A field of fireweed
Summer's waning days passing
Grandchildren growing

Each little flower
Is part of the total Beauty
of the universe

With fireweed swaying
Bees collecting sweet nectar
Honey jars are ready

Sweet Peace

Rounded the curve of a hiking trail,
saw a field of dancing fireweed.

Swaying gently in the breeze—
A kind of heavenly scene.

Bee nuzzling the nectar cup. Sweet
Peace filled my soul.

In the solace of solitude, I closed my eyes.
Heard the bees humming a pleasant lullaby.

I listened until my soul was filled—
Beauty and Grace thrilled.

Anxieties of noisy pandemic world cease.
Peace, sweet Peace!

Fireweed swaying gently in breeze
A heavenly sweet Peace!

*****

Hold fireweed in your soul.
Swaying in the gentle breeze.
Glittering in the radiant sunlight.
Feel the warmth of the rays.
Hold infinity in your heart. Eternity in your soul.

Death is but a flower opening
to shine in another realm.
Like radiant fireweed,
opening on a summer day.
Wild and perfect for a season.
Perishing yet living forever!
Married to Beauty and Wonder—
Peace, sweet Peace!

Come walk
among the fireweed.
Their slender stalks
reaching toward the sun.

They are strong and tenacious,
being the first to come back
after a fire has consumed
all in its path.

Fireweed's deep roots
penetrate below
the Alaska permafrost
that protects the roots from harm.

Teaching us to send deep
tentacles of faith
into the Goodness of God,
enabling us to ward off
the fiery darts of evil.

Walking in fields of fireweed
Inspiration flashes up
as light and sweet
as bees sipping nectar from honey cup.

Responding,
my soul sings
with a music
not of this time and place—
A music of angels.
Singing of heaven's grace.

Glory to God—
In the world and for the world
In us and for us.
Glory to God in the heavens!

(Photo of my wife, Beth, with hat off; and her sister, Janice Green)

Sisters

Flowers in garden
Dan Dan & Mom blossoms
Sweeter than roses

Purple's the color
Of flower garden beauties
Kneel before royalty

Sun kissing moon
Mountains are blushing pink
Flowers are budding
Leaves trembling music
My soul comes awake

(Spring full moon is called the flower moon,
pink moon, and also the worm moon.
The worms are wiggling in the ground.
King salmon appear in Alaska in May.)

Sit among flowers.
Touch tassels of Jesus' robe—
Feel God's love and care.

Sit among flowers.
Touch Mother Teresa's robe—
Care for poor children.

Sit among flowers.
Touch the Buddha's tattered robe—
Teach kindness for all.

D. Cole

Primula denticulate—Common name, drumstick primula.
It is native to Alpine region and gave birth to my poem, Garden Magic.
You can see this and other nature photos and poems in my book, *Kindness Is Every Step: Photos and Poems*.
Nurturing tenderness is a big step toward saving
our environment *and our world.*

Garden Magic

When the world falls apart
keep the memory of a spring garden
where every flower petal
is a little heart.

When the world falls apart
flowers will still be giving.
The birds will still be singing.
Bees will still be humming their part.

All playing a joyful Psalm.
Inviting us to open our soul,
and let the symphony make us whole.
Nature is a praise song.

We must save our gardens.
If everything falls down,
the Spirit will still fly in and out.
In the garden everything is magic!

Tender Kisses

If you do not live in Kindness,
You will dwell where flowers wilt.
Wildflowers thrive by kissing
the soft rays of the morning sun,
and gently sipping the dew drops.

Ode to Spring

Bobbing along in the Bog
On a beautiful spring day!

Grandchildren skipping and singing
Flowers on the path.

We follow in sing-song stride
Joy is everywhere.

Precious treasures
Oh children! Sing for us a song!

Your song and your dance give
Spring to our lives!

(These thoughts came from
walks with grandchildren
from time of kindergarten.
We remember them starting to sing
the Waldorf song, "Spring is coming,"
and we all joined in.)

Kindness is like a flower garden—
It grows best when lovingly nurtured.
God is in nature luring all entities toward
Beauty, Wonder, Goodness,
and healing Kindness.
In this reciprocal relationship,
Kindness blossoms, wafting its sweet perfume
for all to enjoy. Our world,
filled with pain and sadness,
needs more flower gardens.

D. Cole

The teleology of the universe moves
toward Beauty. —Alfred North Whitehead

Seeing With New Eyes

The more we look at Nature
The more She looks back at us

Seeing the small things
Gives more clarity to the big picture

All things become connected
The flowers feed the bees

The bees fertilize the flowers
The bees and the flowers feed us

Fireweed honey is delicious
Lets the Glory shine in

Contemplating nature's wonders
Restores and makes us whole

God is in this mysterious world
Nurturing all things in Beauty

Luring us to become
Our very best selves

Seeing with new eyes—

Transformed by the little bee
We lift our eyes to the heavens

The Great One,
The Mountain of Myth—
Emerges in all Her Glory!

Oh so beautiful
Flowers falling from the sky
They fly up again

D. Cole

Garden Magic

When the world falls apart
keep the memory of a spring garden
where every flower petal
is a little heart.

When the world falls apart
flowers will still be giving.
Birds will still be singing.
Bees will still be humming their part.

All playing a joyful Psalm.
Inviting us to open our soul
and let the symphony make us whole.
Nature is a praise song.

When everything falls apart
Go gently into the garden
the spirit will still be flying in and out.
In the garden everything is music.

Flowers open reaching for the heavens
in each the sun and moon are hidden
each a star poem in which
God whispers Beauty and Love

flowers thrive kissing
soft rays of the morning sun
sipping morning tea

Petals
Sepals
Stamen
Carpel
Stigma
Pistil

Radiant as the sun!

Flowers are easier seen with eyes
than spoken with tongue!

Little flower sun
Imitating is such fun
You brighten my day

Such beauty and intrigue
can not be captured
in one name.

Surprise Lily.
Naked Lady.
Resurrection Lily.

All names indicate
transformation
beyond belief.

This naked lady of the dell
knows her time to shine.
To open her pink bell
in the moonlight sublime.

When the sun rises
she will clothe herself
for she shows her beauty
only in the darkness.

I have felt the surprise
of resurrection birth
as she came forth before sunrise
answering some eternal command.

I know I will live forever
In this virginal birth
and I will never
be quite the same
after this resurrection mirth.

Seeing God

I wake early,
drink my coffee,
eat my fruit and cereal,
and go eagerly into nature.

Like the little lad who stood in my office door,
with hands on hips exclaiming,
"I want to see God, now!"

I go gently into nature,
stand at the portal to look for God.
Mindfully I center on the little things,

Dew drops
hanging from the flower petals
 like sparkling diamond earrings.

Small drops,
but opening a sea of beauty and
meaning. I swim in the depths
and find my soul cleansed and refreshed.

What I questioned in the darkness of the night
tossing in my bed, I now see unfold
in this mystery filled gift of nature
truths foretold.

I have seen God in the dew drops of an early
sunrise!
For in these sparkling gems is the water
that fills the oceans, the air we all breathe,
and God in whom we believe.

My child's request is answered!

D. Cole

Prickly Rose Beauty

Prickly Rose,
with a galaxy of stars
for your heart-shape,
soft velvet-like petals
to enclose.

My eyes feast
on your summer treat,
while sipping tea
from your pink heart
shaped petals.

Cook jelly
from your round
rose hip sister,
but stay away from
the two pronged troublesome seeds.

Make a lei
to give to friends,
from your red winter twigs
and crimson leaves.

Thank you,
Prickly Rose,
for blessing me
with your
year long Beauty.

(This Beauty is found throughout Alaska)

Providing for the Little Ones

Nature has many keys
that unlock the mysteries.

Golden is the lowly cricket
sipping nectar from the water lily cup.

Without regard for race or creed
all are invited to sup.

Nature provides for all
her children in need.

So should we.
So should we.

Nature's fireworks
Dazzling display of light
The Milky Way

Does a honeybee know

the beauty of the flower?

Or does a bee only have a tongue

to taste the nectar of the hour?

The flavor of honey

is of no concern to the bee.

If one only has 45 days to work for the queen

going from lily to lily is as good as it can be.

Garden Grace

I write love notes
to the flower garden,
for she shares with me
her tender petals
and sweet fragrance.

As the flower fades,
their gift of color stays.
My life glows evermore.
Enriched by her colorful
and tender gifts.

I go gently into the garden
to learn from her ways—
Be enlivened by Beauty
that I may treat others
with Kindness and Grace

Secrets of Nature

The one who discovers the secrets of nature—
The wildflowers forever renewing blossoms.
That soul shall rise to meet every danger
and will conquer the last enemy,
death, with the fortitude of faith.

A Song for Everybody

Flowers sing their lullaby songs
for spring rains
and warm sunshine.

Loved ones rocking
in Eternity's arms
come awake
in their melody of love.

And in the sweet perfume
sing for everyone
in a golden heaven.

D. Cole

Truth is Beauty

Beauty is a timeless truth.
Waiting to unfold.
Telling the truth may hurt,
but when done with kindness
it blossoms as a beautiful flower.
That is all we need to know.

(I chose this flower photo for my short poem, Truth is Beauty, for the beauty is unfolding from stony untended soil. Decay is all around. I am afraid that society is sometimes like an untended garden. We hear a lot about lies today, and we often do not know the source of Beauty and Truth.The poem suggests that Kindness is the lamp that reveals True Beauty. Kindness is healing and transforming energy.)

A Song for Everybody

Golden flowers
dressed only in sunlight
come awake,

Sing a song
without words
for everybody.

In the gentle music
loved ones
awake.

Golden heaven
sings a love song
for everybody.

Time stands still
When gazing at flowers
Flowers are forever

I tenderly care for my dicentra spectabilis,
bleeding heart plant,
as a beautiful reminder
to show compassion
for the suffering of others.

The World Becomes a Garden

The morning glories opened
their mouths for the hummingbirds
to caress with fluttering wings
and to kiss delightfully.
Sighing deeply,
the angels blush with envy.
All the world becomes a garden.

Rain Drops:

Raindrops on flower petals
angel's tears of overflowing joy
add to the sparkling jewels.

Tea for green crickets.
Served in a china cup
mixed with golden honey.

Cricket frogs are pleased
to hang out on my welcome mat leaves.
Sipping my attar flavored dew drop tea.

Each drop full of heaven's love
flavored with the compassion
of the centuries.

Some of these drops
first fell
on Moses at Mt. Sinai.

Some evaporated into the air
and fell again in the tears of Jesus
in the Garden of Prayer.

Other droplets traveled
on Galilean pathways to become
wine at the wedding in Cana.

Dripped in blood flowing
from the nail scarred hands of Jesus
on the cross of Calvary.

Sprinkled on child or adult
They become healing Grace
and redeeming love.

Nature's fireworks
Dazzling display of light
The Milky Way

Bee Blessed

If your life is short,
sipping nectar from lilies
is a blessed life.

I sit among the spring flowers.
Hear lullabies of God's care for me.
Rocked in the cradle of kindness.

At Home in Nature

My philosophical bent led me for 50 years,
as a minister in churches
and as an instructor in college and seminary,
to see the big picture—
World view and how God relates to the world.
Retired and living in Alaska
for the last twelve years,
I have gone into the beauty of the mountains
to be still and contemplate—
Paying attention to the small things:
the small black capped chickadees,
nuthatches, and redpolls reveal the wonder of evolution.

I cup a single wildflower and see

the essence of the universe.

The gift of contemplation is in the flower.

In the small things I see the large picture more clearly.

I see God in all things and for all things,

in us and for us, luring us to become our best selves—

Meeting each entity with a Tender care, that nothing is lost.

In the Beauty of nature I see an enduring Love for all things.

My world view grows to understand all things

connected and interrelated.

In these solitary moments I feel at home—

At home with Beauty, Goodness, and Tenderness.

My soul sings alleluia, alleluia!

In my eyes find flowers for your grief
In my heart find relief. D. Cole

Globe shaped bulb
Magically opening in bog
Stars twinkling love

The Master Gardener

God is best seen
as the Tender Master Gardener
Patiently nurturing flowers

The world does not exist apart from God. God the Gardener loves natural beauty. The Gardener, in tenderness, hovers over every flower and whispers, "Awake. Grow. Grow beautiful." Flowers grow, with butterflies flitting and bees humming from red, orange, and yellow flowers. Beautiful gardens answer the call and over eons of time, all nature is lured toward ever enriching possibilities until conditions are right for life forms to emerge. Over billions of years God called forth a world able to support human beings.

Humans are a new song that nature hums, the music swells with each new stanza, giving purpose and meaning. Humans moved from flowers, being gatherers of flowers in the garden, to being gardeners, ever singing nature's love songs. Love, kind acts, and doing the right thing---these are all products of the flower garden within us that we nurture with God's guidance. (Taken from pages 18-19, in my book, *A Relational Hermeneutic of Kindness*).

Breaking News

It is one of the mysteries—

This frail body

houses both sorrow and joy!

On the days the "Breaking News"

is all about death and violence,

I walk slowly in the flower garden.

I bow down often

smelling the sweet fragrance.

My soul feels Goodness and Beauty.

God is best conceived

as a Tender Master Gardener

Patiently Nurturing beautiful flowers.

Conclusion

"To know someone here or there with whom you can feel
there is understanding in spite of distances or thoughts expressed...
That can make life a garden."
—Johann Wolfgang Von Goethe

Do not feel lonely.
the entire universe is inside you.
You are a flower.
Nurtured with Tender care by the Master Gardener.

Rise and Shine

I love how the fireweed
Sends roots deep into the ground
Beyond the permafrost level
After fires burn every thing to the ground
Fireweed is the first flower to return
Hiding its scars and pains
Lifting its sweet purple blossoms
Rising into the blue sky
Becoming one with the sun
Rising and shining bright again
Food for butterflies and bees
Nourishment for the soul
 Inspiring us to send deep roots
Into the soil of faith
Rising and shining bright!

On the tundra—
Fireweed, fireweed blazing red.
Nourishment for bees.

BIRDS AND FLOWERS

Seeing and hearing birds singing,

my brain makes melodic music.

My heart is thankful for the graceful creatures

who dance upon the wind

and make the gentle music of the skies.

Seeing and smelling flowers,

my soul is enraptured.

Siting by the flowers, my spirit says—

"Thank you for the grace of your blossoms,

the sweetness of your breath,

and for sprinkling heaven's colors along my earthly path."

Considering how God cares for the birds and the flowers,

I believe and trust God's care for me.

My prayer is that all will know God's care

and Peace that passes all understanding.

The Meaning of Life

We are all seeking meaning for our lives,
expressed more personally and existentially
as the experience of being alive.

When we walk in nature, we become one with all things.
We experience first hand
the marriage of life and nature.

Marriage thrives on two persons becoming one,
each experiencing
the richness of the other.

If you want to change your life, change the metaphor.
Marriage is a metaphor that changes everything---
the union of oneness.

In the marriage of our soul with nature's soul
all become one with new meaning
and we experience aliveness.

Newness of life is experienced
as I taste with the elves water drops on a flower petal—
The essence of the universe is in that sweetness.

Confucius Creativity

I aspire to walk daily
ascending staircase to heaven—
Higher consciousness.

*****

I aspire to walk daily
ascending staircase to heaven—

Gaining value for my life,
and value for all others.

White and red carnations
on every landing.

Flowers tell secrets
to those who quietly tune in.
Go, be still, listen.

*****

Flower gardens sing secrets,
to those who quietly listen.

Symphonies are playing,
With butterflies and bees humming.

Inviting humans,
to join the heavenly music.

Photo by G.W. Reid

Last Will and Testament

When I die scatter my ashes
in a garden of wildflowers.
Sit in silence among the flowers.
My soul blossoms in garden songs
of butterflies and bees.
Roses speak Kindness for me
and hold you in Love.

Fireweed petals fall
Starlight shines on grassy sod.

Family Love is Forever

When the time comes
that I can't be with you.

Take this book, *When Flowers Speak*,
into a field of fireweed.

Each flower petal will say,
 I'll be in your heart forever.

*****

As you sit among the wildflowers,
I am in the gentle breeze.

I am in the songbird's music.
I am in their swift flight.

Don't weep for my passing.
I am here in the sunlight.

Confucius Creativity

I aspire to walk daily
ascending staircase to heaven—
Higher consciousness.

*****

I aspire to walk daily
ascending staircase to heaven—

Gaining value for my life,
and value for all others.

White and red carnations
on every landing.

(The list of my books on the next page were all born from

my masters thesis, HERMENEUTICAL THEORY IN TRANSITION AS

REFLECTED IN INTERPRETATION: A JOURNAL OF BIBLE

AND THEOLOGY (1947-1966); and my doctoral dissertation,

BAPTISM AND THE LORD'S SUPPER IN THE GOSPEL OF JOHN:

A HERMENEUTICAL INQUIRY. This parentage is especially true of my

book, A Relational Hermeneutic of Kindness. On the deepest level, all of

my 50 year preaching ministry, published articles, Sunday School lessons,

and devotions were born from this parentage. Also, in my poetry I seek to

unite science and the humanities in a clear voice that brings healing to our

broken world.)

OTHER BOOKS BY DWAYNE COLE

A Center that Holds: Adventures in Kindness
Alpenglow Miracles: Fire Dance of Wonder
A Prayer of Blessing: As You Go Remember This
A Relational Hermeneutic of Kindness
A Relational Trinity of Kindness
BEARS AND MOOSE OF ALASKA: Nature Poetry
Clouds of Inspiration
Down on the Farm in Georgia: A Poetic Memoir
Dragonfly Magic
Gentle Galilean Glories: The Tender Teachings of Jesus
God and Evil: An Ode to Kindness
Heart Haiku: Alaska Inspired Photos and Poems
Heart Sijo: Alaska Inspired Photos and Poems
Jesus' Transforming Beatitudes: Selected Sermons from Year A Jesus'
Transforming Love: Selected Sermons from Year B
Jesus' Transforming Gentle Teachings: Selected Sermons from Year C
Kindness Is Every Step
Lone Leaf Dancing
Poems Inspired by Process Philosophy
Poet of the Universe: A Vision of Beauty and Goodness.
The Apostles' Creed: A Living Creed for the Living Church
The Bible: A Poetic Journey
The Book of Revelation: Jesus' Kindness Transforms Suffering
The Serenity Prayer: A Pathway to Peace and Happiness
The Story of the Bible: Authority, Inspiration, Canonization, and Translation
TREES AND DRIFTWOOD: Poetic Ecology
WINGS OF INSPIRATION